RESTORING ARCHITECTURE

THE WORK OF ÁLVARO BARRERA

RESTORING ARCHITECTURE
THE WORK OF ÁLVARO BARRERA

Direction and edition
BENJAMÍN VILLEGAS

Texts
ALBERTO SALDARRIAGA-ROA

Photography
ANTONIO CASTAÑEDA-BURAGLIA

Villegas
editores

This book has been created, edited and
published in Colombia by
VILLEGAS ASOCIADOS S. A.
Avenida 82 No. 11-50, Interior 3
Bogotá D. C., Colombia.
Telephone (57-1) 616 1788
Fax (57-1) 616 0020
e-mail: informacion@VillegasEditores.com

Art department
Arch. OLGA LUCÍA NOVOA

Proof reader
STELLA DE FEFERBAUM

English translation
JIMMY WEISKOPF

First edition
October, 2003

ISBN
958-8156-34-3

Collaboration in the design of the projects in Cartagena and direction of the
works of restoration: the architect GLORIA PATRICIA MARTÍNEZ.

Collaboration in the design of projects:
The architect HUMBERTO GÓMEZ (Casa Calle del Curato)
The architect PIEDAD GÓMEZ (Hotel Santa Teresa, Casa Pestagua)
The architect BILLY GOBERTUS (Casa Calle de los Estribos)
The architect CLAUDIA HERNÁNDEZ (Casa de la Hacienda Montes,
Hotel de la Ópera, Hotel Santa Teresa)
The architect MARIANA PATIÑO (Casa Liévano)
The engineer AUGUSTO ESPINOSA (San Agustín)
The architects ÁLVARO MORENO and NORHA PIEDRAHITA
(Casa de los Barcos).
The engineer JOSÉ RAÚL LONDOÑO (Lighting design)
The architect ÁLVARO ANDRÉS BARRERA (Old Hospital of Santa Marta, House
on the Calle de las Damas, House on the east coast of Panama and computer
models)

ÁLVARO BARRERA wishes to thank:
The architect GLORIA PATRICIA MARTÍNEZ, who was his pupil, collaborator
and partner in the works in Cartagena for fifteen years

VillegasEditores.com

TABLE OF CONTENTS

RESTORATION AS ARCHITECTURE

A conversation between Álvaro Barrera-Herrera
and Alberto Saldarriaga-Roa

A.S.R. —The history of the interventions in Colombia's architectural heritage has still not been written. Álvaro Barrera-Herrera has had a long and polemical role in this story. His earliest work as a restorer was carried out under the auspices of the Corporación Nacional de Turismo (the National Corporation of Tourism), an entity that no longer exists, which sponsored several important projects in different parts of the country.
In 1968 the creation of the Instituto Colombiano de Cultura ("Colcultura", the Colombian Institute of Culture) led to an inventory of historic monuments and later its Heritage section assumed a more direct responsibility for the protection of the country's architectural heritage. Álvaro Barrera was the head of this section between 1974 and 1982, a period that is considered epoch-making in the history of Colombian culture, at the time when Gloria Zea was the director of the Institute. It was in those years that the concept of a "heritage" acquired importance in the cultural language of the country.

A.B.H. —From the time of its creation in 1968, the National Corporation of Tourism had been the entity responsible for the largest number of restorations in the country. A very important one was the intervention in the Quinta de San Pedro Alejandrino near the city of Santa Marta (the country estate where Bolívar passed his final days). In 1974, the Heritage section of the Colombian Institute of Culture proposed a series of initiatives, barely developed at the time, that had to do with making an inventory of our cultural heritage, training architectural restorers and administering the heritage on a small budget.
To solve the latter problem, a team was formed with the Banco de la República (the Central Bank), and the Foundation for the Conservation and Restoration of the Colombian Cultural Heritage was created. The joint work of the two institutions resulted in a period of intensive work in the rescue of this heritage.
It counted upon the collaboration of first-class restorers, like Jaime Salcedo, who was responsible for the project involving the convento de Monguí, an old Jesuit monastery located in the department of Boyacá. One of the first works directly promoted by the Heritage section was the recuperation of the monastery of San Agustín, also in Boyacá, which was in danger of being demolished as a "ruin". Colcultura sponsored the project and the Foundation put up the money. This was my first job with a building of great historic value.

A.S.R. —The restoration of the convento de San Agustín was a noteworthy project from the very beginning, especially because of the use of contemporary materials, like the iron used in the replacement of the missing arches of the cloister. This work may now be seen as a sort of "manifesto" of your stance on restoration.

A.B.H. —The restoration of the San Agustín monastery presented the challenge of working with a ruined structure which had great gaps in its arcades and interior walls. In this project

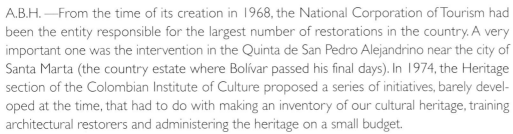

Aerial perspective

risky decisions were made, in accordance with the needs of the building, the basic principles of restoration and the design that we wanted to incorporate into it.

In this sense it was a personal manifesto. It would have been possible to replace the missing arches by imitating the existing ones, since the model which served for the copy was there. Instead of choosing this type of intervention, we replaced them with new arches, made of iron rods, which were curved "in the creole manner" by the local foundrymen who dared to do it. The existing gaps in the walls were left intact and strengthened, and large windows were inserted in them. The structural solution for the seismic resistance of these gaps was found by the engineer Augusto Espinosa, who did the calculations and drew the design. It has turned out to be a successful one, since it has stood up to several earthquakes without being affected.

Another interesting intervention in the cloister of San Agustín was the recuperation of the mural painting, which was achieved with the help of Rodolfo Vallín, who had arrived from Mexico to participate in the teaching activities of the National Restoration Center. From this point of view, the works of "restoration", in the strict sense of the word, were carried out with complete rigor. The presence of the metallic arches and the large glass windows, that is, of a contemporary language in a colonial cloister, was controversial: it was widely discussed, but finally recognized to be valid.

Since then I have faced problems in which the decisions I have had to take are not simply a matter of restoring this or that part of building but of assuming a personal position with regard to a building that incorporates different kinds of interventions.

A.S.R. —After nearly two centuries of debate, throughout the world, on the handling of the architecture of the past, there is still a lack of agreement about the correct way to intervene in mankind's architectural heritage. Given the differences of opinion and criteria that are found among those who practice the restoration of works of architecture, not only in Colombia but also in the rest of the world, one comes to the conclusion that there are no absolute norms for this work. How, then, do you train a restorer?

A.B.H. —Those of us who undertook the first works of restoration in Colombia did not have an official title of "restorer". Some of us had taken courses in Spain and Italy, thanks, among other things, to the scholarships that were available in those years. A good part of the experience accumulated in Colombia in the past thirty years is owed to the "non-restorers". Nowadays a new generation of professionals has arisen, people who have done postgraduate studies and have a Master's degree in the field of restoration. This significantly changes the employment situation, but at bottom the problems are the same.

Intervention in the architectural heritage requires much more than an accumulation of technical knowledge – in the end it is a question of architecture. An architect who is knowledge-

Floor plan

able about the history of architecture - in his own country and on a world level - and who has architectural ideas is qualified to work on buildings of the past. You don't have to be a specialist. A knowledge of restoration techniques helps, but it is not everything.

This knowledge is found among craftsmen, who often know more than the architect. A good engineer who understands the vulnerability of old buildings is essential. But the person who organizes the works as a whole is the architect. It is possible to give a technical training to a restorer, but difficult to give him a conceptual one.

For this reason it is also difficult to speak of "schools" that train restorers. The concepts do not derive from the techniques but from the architect's knowledge and sense of history. If an idea of architecture does not exist in the intervention in the heritage, the problem is reduced to a technical and stylistic imitation of the past.

A.S.R. —Restoration is usually regarded as a discipline that is different to and on occasions separate from architecture. For many people the word *restoration* indicates a technique rather than a body of knowledge. For others it is a science. From a certain point of view, it is more convenient to speak of an intervention in buildings with a cultural value than of restoration. There are different positions with regard to these kinds of interventions, some more orthodox than others.

The very idea of orthodoxy has variations. Some people are afraid of copying or counterfeiting, others of being too contemporary. There is agreement on such aspects as the use of rigorous techniques of restoration for this or that material or part of a building, but there are doubts about the overall focus of a work.

In all this an important question arises - why restore a building? The most obvious answer is to prolong its existence and conserve its presence in a form that it is as close as possible to its original state. The first assertion is true, the second is ambiguous. A material relic is inevitably subject to deterioration. Giving it the possibility of surviving the passage of time is a valid enterprise and requires specialized knowledge.

The second is somewhat relative. In each moment of their lives, buildings have responded to the needs of their inhabitants and have often undergone substantial changes in appearance. Some of those changes acquire a historical value, in many cases it is impossible to return to the origin.

Another important problem is updating old buildings so that they meet the requirements of contemporary life. A building's original uses are replaced by new ones, many with special demands of convenience, environmental comfort and modern installations. There are also other implications.

What kind of appearance should the restored building have? Should it look old? Should it look new or renovated? Modern life is not merely a matter of installing public services in a house. There is something more.

Cross section

A.B.H. —To undertake a job of intervention in a work of architecture you need to understand its characteristics and act appropriately.

Some buildings are unique, they are landmarks of architecture which also have a use that will endure over time. An ancient church, for example, has unique values that should be conserved "to the letter".

The objective is to give these monuments an enduring life in the best possible conditions, without altering their character.

There are other buildings, that, for one reason or another, need to be adapted to new uses and requirements which are characteristic of contemporary life. In these cases the architect proposes ideas which, in addition to recuperating the essential values of the building, turn the intervention into something special, suitable to the aims that are foreseen. In these cases you have to make the past live alongside the present, give dynamism to the building, project it over time, give it new life. Restoration techniques are combined with contemporary interventions, without losing sight of the matter of character, which is what finally defines the overall result.

A.S.R. —Most of Álvaro Barrera's work involves the restoration of old houses, so that they may be used today as homes. In a certain way this is a specialty. The houses continue to be what they were, houses, but their character is transformed.

A.B.H. —Curiously, it is in the field of the house that a heritage intervention presents the greatest conceptual problems. This will surely be denied by many restorers. As I said, intervening in a building of a monumental character involves problems of size, but in the end it is a matter of making the building the same as it was.

There are clearly defined criteria. You have to consolidate the structure and recuperate its values. There isn't scope for many conceptual proposals. In a residential building there are many factors to consider and one of these is the well-being it may offer to its inhabitants. It is widely accepted that a contemporary intervention in historic buildings should introduce elements that did not exist in the past, for example, electricity, toilets and in some cases, air conditioning. In colonial homes there was none of that. There were no toilets, the use of the spaces was different. Nowadays a home without these facilities would be unacceptable. But there is a lot of debate about other kinds of interventions, for example, the use of color and new materials or the introduction of swimming pools. In the colonial period they did not exist either.

You have to put a lot of thought into making a house habitable. The problem is not only one of interior design. Many people commission a work of restoration and then call on an interior designer to finish the job. That is not my idea of how it should be done.

Interior view

14

A.S.R. —Álvaro Barrera has carried out interventions in a large number of colonial houses in Cartagena de Indias. The city, founded in 1537 by Pedro de Heredia, was included, in 1984, in the Unesco list of places that form the Cultural Patrimony of Mankind.

In each district of the old city there was a characteristic kind of house. The "high" two-storey houses, some of them with an "*entresuelo*" (mezzanine), an intermediate floor that only occupies part of the front of the house and which was used as a storeroom or warehouse, are found in the district of Santo Domingo. In the neighborhoods of San Diego and Getsemaní "low" one-storey houses predominate.

The layout of a typical colonial house in Cartagena consists of a main patio facing the entrance hall (*zaguán*), surrounded by three sections, a front, side and rear one. In some cases you find central patios that are surrounded by four sections. In others you only find the front and the side body. Originally there were gardens full of vegetation in the interior of the properties.

Many colonial houses were subjected to interventions at the end of the 19th and the beginning of the 20th centuries. These interventions are known as "republican" ones, a term used to specify the stylistic characteristics of the ornamentation superposed on the old structures. Years later some houses were "modernized" and there appear works in cement and reinforced concrete.

A.B.H. —One of the sources of the colonial house of Cartagena was the Andalusian house of the 16th and 17th centuries. That house arose from the specific climatic conditions of Andalusia and its particular cultural heritage. In Cartagena, during the colonial period, adjustments were made to this model, which responded, among other things, to the conditions of a humid tropical climate. The same thing occurred in other parts of the Caribbean. From the start, the regional spirit rebelled against the manner of living imposed by the model.

The patio was the center of life in the colonial house of Cartagena. Watchtowers were built above the roofs to observe the arrival of ships. The gardens full of vegetation located at the rear of the houses were their inner landscape. The architecture was enlivened by color. Later on, in the 19th and at the beginning of the 20th centuries, the appearance of the houses changed. Ornamentation that was previously unknown emerged. Afterwards, many houses in the historic center were abandoned and fell into a state of deterioration.

Given that the essence of the Cartagena house is introverted, when I intervene in one I consider it indispensable to create an interior world that offers pleasant sensations to its inhabitants. Those who inhabit one of these houses want to feel the presence of the tropics in the vegetation and water, in the heat and coolness, in the light and penumbra. The entrance patio is a space that acquires a special importance in this private world. It no longer needs to be bare and arid, it can be the center of enjoyment in the house.

There I combine plants and water in different ways. The watchtower, which formerly had a practical purpose, is now a space for contemplating the sea from the private world of each

Typical traditional balcony

17

person. I have placed swimming pools or basins in the terraces and watchtowers that exist there. All of this has led to a lot of polemics among restorers.

There are many kinds of colonial houses in Cartagena, some large and imposing, others small and simple. The intervention in a small house is as important as the one that is done in a big house. Many of the houses of Cartagena on which I have worked were deteriorated or were of minor importance in terms of their historical value for the city. In some cases the intervention has followed "the letter of the law", in others I have proposed ideas that are daring from the point of view of conventional restoration. But in all of them an attempt has been made to achieve a special character, something that makes them unique for their owners.

A.S.R. —When you intervene in old constructions you find materials that are no longer being produced, which were handled with building techniques that, on occasions, have now been forgotten. For one reason or another it is necessary to introduce new materials that are handled with contemporary techniques. For years there was the idea that a restored property had to look new. The old plaster of lime and sand was replaced by a new one of cement. There was not much interest in historical accuracy, a renovated appearance was preferred. When you explore a building you find all sorts of vestiges: fragments of the original floors, mural paintings hidden behind layer upon layer of paint, traces of colors that were used in the past and can be employed in the present. On certain occasions there are singular details which give the building character and which need to be highlighted.

A.B.H. —The needs and demands of the contemporary world require interventions that were unthinkable before. One of them, which is very important, is to strengthen the bearing structure of the building. You need to tie the walls of the house with elements that work through compression, for example, tie beams in reinforced concrete. You also need to restore the wooden structures of the roofs.

The original timber is no longer available and it is an ecological sin to sacrifice a forest in order to fix up a house. In this case the conservation of one part of our heritage may imply the destruction of another part. You thus need to establish criteria to know how to introduce new materials in such repairs. The restoration of an ancient wall is a delicate job, it requires compatible materials and techniques. Other interventions accept the use of new materials. In the San Agustín monastery in Tunja the plaster that had fallen from the adobe walls was replaced with one of lime and sand. A careful examination was made of the walls. The paint that had been superposed on the walls over the years was eliminated and the oldest layers were left, which also allowed for the rescue of remains of the mural paintings.

The new plaster was painted with lime mixed with mineral pigments similar to the original colors. For that reason the walls showed stains, which was not common in restored works at that time. A restored building had to look new. In San Agustín the ancient was made evident.

Church of San Andrés de Pisimbalá

Color has been a controversial element in the interventions done to historic buildings. At one time, it was officially decided that the whole of the colonial and republic heritage of Colombia should be white and that norm was imposed in many historic centers.

The first problems with the use of color appeared in the works done, under the auspices of the National Corporation of Tourism, in the cloister of the Seminary of San Juan Nepomuceno and the Quinta de San Pedro Alejandrino in the city of Santa Marta. In both buildings the original yellow ochre was restored. The justification for these decisions was found in historical documents, for example, the watercolors of Edwark Mark, which showed what San Pedro Alejandrino looked like in 1845. Jaime Salcedo, who was in charge of this restoration project, did a thorough job of research and his idea about the colors could not be refuted.

When I was working in Colcultura, at nearly the same time as the work on San Agustín in Tunja I was in charge of the restoration of the "casa Liévano", which was one of the seats of the Institute. This is a house with a lot of "republican" ornamentation, located in the historic center of Bogotá, near the Plaza de Bolívar. There were no precedents for intervention in the domestic architecture of the republican period, which was not to the liking of a number of historians and restorers. The colonial heritage had monopolized interest before that time and the value of republican architecture was just beginning to be understood.

In the intervention in the façade of the casa Liévano we used a combination of pale green and different tones of red. As it was thought that the historic center of Bogotá should be white, the new look of this house caused a scandal.

The official in charge of that district of the city made me stop the job. This and other works gave rise to a controversy about the appearance of historic buildings in the center of Bogotá and finally the use of color won out.

Something similar occurred with the first intervention in a house in Cartagena, located in the Calle de Don Sancho. There had been a fire in the house and the roofs were missing. On the interior walls and the façade the original colors were found. On the façade we only cleaned the walls and repaired the missing plaster. In some of the interior spaces the colors that had been found were left exposed. The stained appearance of the past that resulted was disliked by historians and restorers at the time. Now it is accepted without reservations.

In heritage places, once the restorable is restored the rest is contemporary intervention. One seeks to place value on the character given by the original colors and on that basis work the other colors. The decision about what color to use derives from an examination of the building and also from chromatic criteria that are applied to the whole project. I usually use mineral pigments mixed with lime. This is a very ancient technique which may be reproduced and even improved today.

A.S.R. —At a simple glance there are cross-references between heritage interventions and new works. In the former contemporary elements are introduced, while in the latter tradi-

Interior view of house
on east coast of Panama

tional materials and techniques are occasionally employed. The old and the new unite in a formal and technical repertory.

A.B.H. —New works in historical buildings should be presented as such. For that reason it is completely valid to introduce contemporary elements, for example, metal staircases or bridges. In some new works I have employed adobe walls to show the contemporary utility of one of the materials that is characteristic of Colombian vernacular architecture. In Peru and Mexico important investigations have been undertaken about earth constructions, with interesting results that are applicable to the improvement of the material's response to damp and stresses. I am also interested in evoking something of the spatiality of colonial houses in contemporary terms. But I do not seek to imitate the past, neither in historical buildings nor in contemporary ones.

A.S.R. —In the work of Álvaro Barrera, there are elements that are common to both restorations and new buildings: vaults, bridges, the employment of water, the use of metal, contrasts between old and new elements. There is also an expressive interest in making a house a special work. There are recurring themes and novelties. Restoration has been interpreted as architecture and in the reverse sense, architecture is understood as evocation. The overall result is a diverse oeuvre that conserves a fundamental unity.

Detail of the church of San Agustín

THE COLONIAL HOUSE OF CARTAGENA

Alberto Saldarriaga-Roa

The colonial houses of Cartagena form part of the extensive family of Latin American domestic architecture developed during the period when the Spanish crown ruled a good part of this continent. They share characteristics similar to those of colonial houses in other parts of the Caribbean and have features of their own which give them a particular architectural identity. The oldest houses date back to the end of the 16th and the beginning of the 17th centuries. Almost all of them were altered in the following centuries.

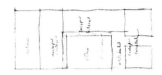

The arrangement whereby the building is placed on the front of the property, facing the street, and has an interior garden ("*solar*"), covered by vegetation, in the rear part forms the basis of the plan of the colonial house of Cartagena. The home is formed by the joining of "bodies" or "sections" ("*cuerpos*" or "*tramos*"), arranged around one or several patios. The front body or section, as its name indicates, is that which shows its face to the city. The following sections are placed within the interior of the property, reaching to the rear boundary of the garden. The main patio is the element which determines the ordering of the house. The position of this patio may be central, or lateral to the entrance, at the end of the entrance hall ("*zaguán*"). The lateral or side patio is surrounded by three sections, one frontal, one lateral and one in the rear. The central patio is surrounded by four constructed sections.

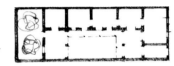

One enters the house through the "*zaguán*" that leads to the vestibule, where the stairway stands, in the case of the two-storey house. The corridors that surround the patio are the spaces that connect what are, strictly speaking, the rooms, which are arranged in a row. The colonial house of Cartagena thus has two typical shapes, a "U" and an "O". These shapes are seen both in one- and two-storey homes.

There are several types of two-storey colonial houses in Cartagena. The most elaborate is the "high" house with a "mezzanine" ("*entresuelo*"), with a side patio and a central entrance, characteristic of the leading merchants of the city. The mezzanine is a second-storey placed over the front and lateral section and connected by a bridge above the entrance hall. The most common high house does not have this mezzanine. In both cases the stairway is located on one of the sides of the ground floor vestibule. The main salon occupies part or whole of the front of the second floor and has a balcony that projects over the street. This salon has a steeply sloping roof, whose wooden structure follows the system known as "*par y nudillo*" with highly elaborate horizontal tie-beams. The one-storey or "low" house is usually made up of three sections grouped around a side patio. The entrance and the entrance hall, which are also lateral, lead to a vestibule with arches that open onto the patio. As in the high house, the central salon is found in the front section, facing the street, and has a similar roof. The long windows stand out from the façade and have what the people of Cartagena call "a belly" ("*panza*"), the protruding base for the very ornate wooden grilles

The smallest houses are known as "annexes" ("*accesorias*"). They have a narrow front, a single section at the front and a single space with a steeply sloping roof held up by very simple wooden structures.

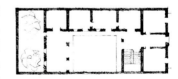

Floor plans and cross sections of a typical colonial Cartagena house

RESTORATION

CONVENTO DE SAN AGUSTÍN

Tunja 1978/1984

The conventual seat was finished in 1603. After 1822, the monastery was used for other purposes, including a jail, and wound up in ruins. It has a very large central patio, one side of which is completely occupied by the church; an "imperial" stairway of three arms which links the two floors; rich ornamentation on the columns and semi-circular arches which border the patio; and a church with a single aisle, a transept, a presbytery and two lateral chapels. Its receded façade forms a small atrium space. A bell-wall tops the façade. The monastery was dynamited and a bit more than half of its structure was left standing. An examination of the surviving sections resulted in the discovery of the orginal roofs with their wooden trusses and cane ceilings, the adobe walls and the mural paintings.

The roof structure of the church was conserved, as well as remains of the barrel vault of its interior, built in the 18th century, with rib-vault arches and the colored coats of arms painted on its imposts. Numerous vestiges of the jail remained. The restoration team found the original floors of the patio, colors of the columns of the arcades and innumerable mural painting. The restoration project sought to free the monastery of elements that were alien to the original structure, leaving, however, some relics of the later interventions. The consolidation of the structure and the straightening of the adobe walls was one of the first jobs. The missing arcade in the main patio was rebuilt in steel. The original stone columns were plastered and painted red, thus their appearance was conserved. The missing sections of the adobe walls of the interior corridors were replaced with big panes of tempered glass. Special interventions were carried out in the interior of the church so that it would serve as a library. The interior vault, which was almost completely destroyed, was reconstructed. To display this reconstruction a metallic mesh covered with transparent plastic was employed. Later, the vault was coated with a plaster of lime and sand. The cells that were found in the space where the presbytery had been were conserved as book stacks. The mural paintings were restored. The original yellow coats of plaster were left exposed. The original floors were restored and the missing ones were replaced with similar materials.

Plan of ground floor

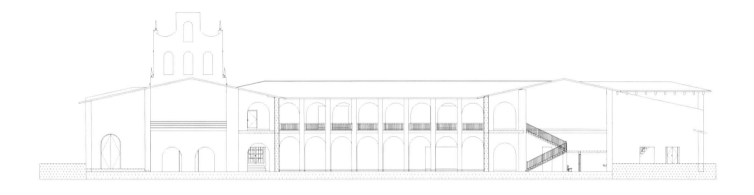

HOUSE ON CALLE DE DON SANCHO

Cartagena 1982

This was the first work of restoration carried out in Cartagena. The two-storey house, which dates back to the 17th century, was destroyed by a fire. It was a ruin, covered by vegetation, when it was acquired. The floor plan adopts the typical "U" form with a side patio. In this case there is no side section, properly speaking, only a corridor which joins the front and rear sections. At the back of the property a large water cistern ("*aljibe*") had been conserved. The watchtower of the house, by contrast, had been almost entirely destroyed.

The intervention aimed at converting the spaces of the house into a group of four apartments. Most of the work was devoted to the recuperation of the surviving features of the original structure and the reconstruction of missing ones, like the watchtower, of which vestiges remained. The work done on the house was novel in Cartagena at that time, though it followed precedents established in the restoration of the San Agustín monastery of Tunja, for example, the recuperation of the original plaster and colors of the house. The gaps in the walls were left exposed, with the black smoke-stains from the fire.

Mural paintings done in the 19th century, which imitated wall paper, were also restored. The roof structure, especially that of the main salon of "*par y nudillo*" with knot-work patterns was completely rebuilt, following the design evidenced by the remains of the charred timber. The salon had vestiges of the black and white checkerboard marble floor, which was reconstructed with demolition materials.

Plan of main façade

HOUSE ON CORNER OF CALLE DE DON SANCHO
AND CALLE DE LA MANTILLA
("HOUSE OF THE SHIPS")

Cartagena 1984

This is a first-class example of the "high colonial house with a mezzanine," characteristic of the wealthy merchants of Cartagena de Indias. It forms part of a group of four houses which have the same doorways, all with the same coat of arms.

The house has a typical "U"-shaped floor plan with a side patio. On both streets the ground floor was originally used for shops and part of the servants' quarters. The mezzanine served as a warehouse and the owners lived on the second floor. Like other merchants' houses, this one had a watchtower. Before the intervention, the structure was found to be nearly complete but on the point of collapse.

The house was subdivided into four independent apartments. The large salon of the second floor was turned into a communal area of the complex. The restoration was very strict and special attention was paid to the recuperation of the original elements and the establishment of a clear distinction between them and the new elements that were required. The watchtower was completely reconstructed. The work was done in stages: each section was worked on separately, without jeopardizing the stability of the rest of the house.

One of the most interesting aspects of this work is the recuperation and restoration of the nearly 200 drawings of ships found on the walls of the house. One of them, the drawing of an Italian galleon, is dated "1780" and is highly elaborate.

HOUSE ON CALLE GASTELBONDO

Cartagena 1986

When it was acquired, the house had been abandoned and was in a ruinous state. The accumulated rubble of many years filled nearly the whole of the ground floor. It lacked a roof and only a number of vestiges of its structure remained. Its floor plan is typical of the colonial period: a side patio with three sections around it. At the beginning of the 20th century it was transformed into the republican style. Several works in cement remained from this remodeling: the floors, the railings and "tejadillo" or "little roof" of the main balcony on the façade, and the moldings that border the arches of the ground floor and the windows of the second floor, around the main patio.

All of the rubble on the ground floor had to be removed before the work could begin. This freed a stone column that was coated in cement, which was restored. A new, completely free-standing main stairway was placed in the space of the original one. The main salon of the second floor was rebuilt with a traditional structure based on the vestiges that were found and it was turned into the main bedroom. In the lateral section, a terrace-watchtower was formed, partly covered by a wooden pergola. The ruins of the rear section were conserved and the borders of the window openings were covered in cement. A swimming pool, placed in the main patio, was introduced into this ruin, incorporating the original water cistern of the house.

The floor and the cement "tejadillo" (little roof) of the main balcony were conserved. The original balustrades were replaced by a number of new wooden ones with the same design, thus conserving the republican appearance.

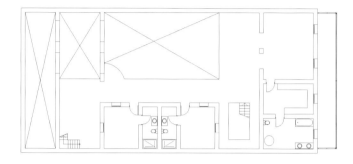

HOUSE ON CORNER OF CALLE LA MANTILLA
WITH CALLE DEL CURATO

Cartagena 1988

This two-storey corner house has a central entrance, a side patio and a wooden corner balcony with a diagonal wooden bracket, a detail that is only found in a few houses in the historic center of the city. It was occupied by the offices of a newspaper for a while and had undergone a lot of intervention by the time it was acquired for conversion into a residence. The front section, the main stairway and the semi-circular arches that border the patio on the ground floor were found in an acceptable state, which allowed for their complete restoration. The rest of the house was in a middling condition.

The open stores on the front of the house were conserved and its interior was subdivided into two apartments. One of them occupies the second floor of the front section, the other makes use of the other two sections. The social areas of the latter apartment were placed on the ground floor, around the patio where the swimming pool was placed. A new stairway leads to the bedrooms on the second floor, which are connected by a corridor with a wooden structure that projects over the patio. The main bedroom is located on the third floor and above it there is a terrace-watchtower.

HOUSE ON CALLE DE LA ESTRELLA

Cartagena 1989/1990

This house has a central patio surrounded by three sections, one frontal and two lateral; one of the latter extends to the rear of the property. The house lacks a garden, which indicates that the property was subdivided at some time in the past. The colonial structure was found to be in an acceptable state of conservation. In the 20th century the original doorways of the façade were converted into semi-circular arches bordered by cement moldings. The original windows were also transformed and were given the "cup" shape that is characteristic of homes in other sectors of the city. Concrete "tejadillos" (little roofs) were built over the lateral balconies of the second floors. All of these interventions were conserved and integrated into the restoration project.

The intervention was limited to recovering the original features of the colonial structure and the only addition was a flat roof in the back part of the patio, which is partly upheld by a surviving pilaster. The terrace which is thus formed serves as a bridge between the two lateral sections. The swimming pool that occupies part of the main patio is placed beneath this terrace.

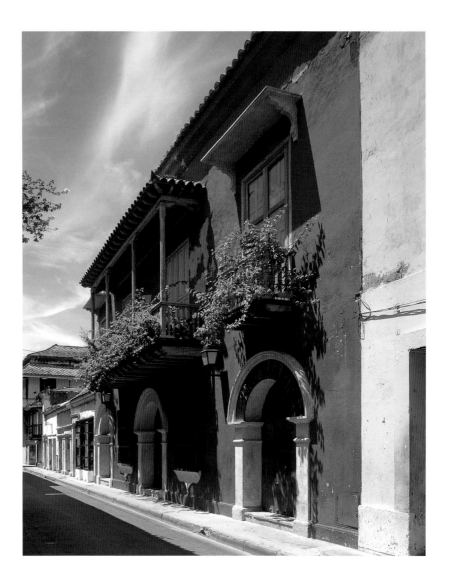

Cross-section plan

50

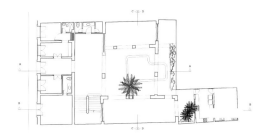

HOUSE ON CALLE TUMBAMUERTOS

Cartagena 1991

The front section of this "low" house with an entrance hallway and side patio was found to be in a relatively good state of conservation. It also had a lateral section covered by a zinc roof and a temporary structure on the second floor of the rear section. The colonial water cistern in the patio was intact. The restoration work concentrated on the front section, which was turned into the main salon after the "*par e hilera*" roof structure was rebuilt. Two bedrooms were placed on the ground floor of the lateral section and the dining room and kitchen at the back of the patio. A stairway built into the side of the patio leads to the main bedroom on the second floor, which is separated from the front section by a terrace which is partly covered by a wooden pergola. From this terrace another stairway branches off to a terrace-watchtower placed above the main bedroom. In the patio the small swimming pool next to the stairway incorporates the house's old water cistern.

HOUSE ON CALLE TUMBAMUERTOS

Cartagena 1992

A special feature of this one-storey house, located in the San Diego sector, is that it stands above the level of the street. It has a typical floor plan, consisting of a front, a lateral and a rear section, arranged around a patio in which the original water cistern of the house was found. The front section was covered with cement roof tiles. The house has windows with projecting tribunes and cement balustrades, which take advantage of its elevated position above the street.

The intervention rebuilt the front section, delimited by an entrance hallway, which was turned into the living room. The original slope of the roof of this section was restored and the cement tiles were replaced by ceramic ones. The rear slope of this roof was raised to make room for a studio on the second floor, located above the old vestibule of the house. In the rear part of the property a new bedroom block was built. The basin was placed on one side of the patio and the old water cistern was incorporated into it.

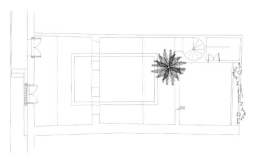

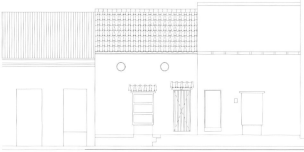

Plan of first floor and main façade

HOUSE ON CALLE DEL CURATO

Cartagena 1992

The front section and part of the walls of the lateral and rear sections of this one-storey house were the basis of the restoration work, which converted it into a residence. Two features of the original layout were wholly conserved: the lateral entrance hall, ending in an arch that opens onto the modest patio, and the salon. A second floor was added to the rear section and separated from the front of the house by a lateral terrace, which covers the space of a dining room that completely opens onto the small patio. The two bedrooms are located on the two floors of the rear section and are joined by a stairway situated in a corner of the patio.

HOUSE ON CALLE DE LA MANTILLA

Cartagena 1992/1993

This two-storey house with a side patio had received a lot of intervention. The main patio had been covered and the main stairway removed. In the preparatory study for its conversion into a residence the original elements that were worth being conserved and restored were identified. It was necessary to place a new main stairway on the site of the original one. The rear section was covered by a flat slab to form a terrace.

The wall of the side patio, which serves as the backdrop for the basin, was raised to conceal the uneven height of the wall that forms the boundary with the adjoining property. It was refaced in "military" brick, handmade in the town of Bayunca, near Cartagena.

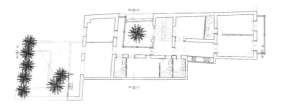

First and second floors

HOUSE ON CALLE DE SANTO DOMINGO

Cartagena 1992/1993

The front section, with the entrance hall and the main space, and a part of the lateral section of this one-storey house were the basis of the design of the project which turned it into a residence. Remnants of the previous structure – a number of square, unroofed pillars and fragments of the rear wall that separated the house from the garden – were incorporated into the new interventions.

One of the intentions of this project was to reconstruct the traditional spatiality of a house with a side patio. The front section and the remains of the lateral section were restored and turned into a living room, dining room and kitchen. A new, "L"-shaped section, of two stories, was constructed in the rear part of the property and houses the bedrooms. The existing pillars in the intermediate space between the two sections were used to support the wooden beams which form a pergola above an informal, open-air dining room. The ruined wall was shored up and part of it was incorporated into the swimming pool that is built into one side of the patio.

The metal columns, beams, railings and roof recreate the traditional style of construction in the new section.

CORNER HOUSE, CALLE DE LA MANTILLA

Cartagena 1993/1994

This corner house is an outstanding example of the colonial merchants' houses which had shops on the ground floor front and living quarters on the second. It originally had a central patio surrounded by four sections, one of which may have communicated with the neighboring property. The large main stairway is located on one side of the main entrance and faces a second one on the other side of the patio, which is approached through an arched corridor. This rear stairway leads to the watchtower, one of the oldest in Cartagena. On the ground floor, on either side of this second stairway, two great vaulted water cisterns had been built. The bridge formed by the roof of the central corridor, a characteristic feature of traditional Arab-influenced Mediterranean architecture, is nearly unique in Cartagena. The big living room was placed on the second floor, near the corner and above the entrance. The bedrooms were aligned along the front, the dining room was placed in the interior lateral wing and the original kitchen was built into one side of it, near the cisterns that supplied it. On this floor, in the vestibule of the stairway, two "Mudéjar" arches of special architectural interest were found.

The façade conserved two original balconies, one built on the corner. The ground floor arches are not original: they date back to the beginning of the 20th century. The house, which had been used for cheap lodging for a number of years, was in a pretty deteriorated state when the intervention work began, which sought, above all, to free the old structure from alterations contrary to the original uses of the house. The ground floor stores were thus conserved and the living quarters were placed on the second floor, in line with the original arrangement. The surviving mural paintings in the stairway were restored and drawings of two ships were discovered in the second-storey corridors. The watchtower was restored. The swimming pool is crossed by the arches of the central corridor and enters into the water cisterns, which were opened to spatially integrate them with the whole grouping. The floor of the central bridge was replaced by a metal framework, which allows light to enter the patio. Another metal bridge joins the watchtower to the dining room terrace.

Plan of first floor

HOTEL SANTA TERESA DE JESÚS

Cartagena 1994/1995

The Santa Teresa convent of Cartagena was founded in the 17th century and occupied a property situated in front of the fortified walls of the district adjoining the plaza of San Pedro Claver. The building originally had two cloistered patios. The convent later served as a police barracks, candle factory, hospital and high school, successively. The front and one of the patios were demolished around 1920. Of the original building, only the arcades on the ground floor of the second patio, a number of lateral walls, and the perimeter and façade of the church had been conserved. A three-storey concrete building, with columns that lacked iron reinforcement bars, was built over the arcades of the patio.

This building was never finished and the only feature worth rescuing was its republican façade on the calle de Ricaurte, which was the same height as the bell-wall of the old church. The empty space in front of the property which had resulted from its demolition was later incorporated into the public spaces of the city. The two-storey house adjacent to the convent also dates back to the 17th century. The central patio with its arcades and some walls on both floors of the building had survived. This house was incorporated into the property of the old convent and integrated into the design of the five-star hotel which was the object of this intervention. It obviously aimed at the conservation and restoration of all of the surviving features of the original buildings, especially the colonial walls and arcades of the patios and the republican façade. The latter determined the overall height of the façades and of the interior of the patio, around which were placed the areas of circulation and the bedrooms of the hotel. Because of its poor quality, the existing concrete structure was demolished and replaced by a new one in steel, which conserved the previous heights of the first and third floors. The space of the second floor of the old building was divided in half and an upper floor, set back from the façades, was constructed. A swimming pool and a cafeteria, covered by a detachable wooden structure, were placed on the terrace on this floor. The old church was turned into a conference hall. The wall of the main altar was adorned with a reproduction of the original altar-piece.

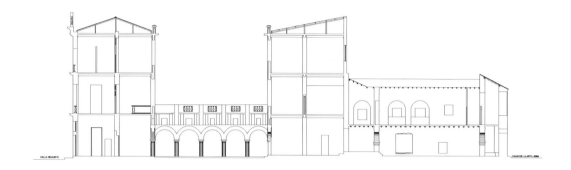

HOUSE ON CALLE DE SANTO DOMINGO

Cartagena 1994/1995

This is another important example of a Cartagena colonial house with two stories and a mezzanine. Built on a very long property, the house originally had three sections arranged around a side patio. Another lateral body with a flat roof was added in the republican period to form the present central patio. A flat wooden ceiling with a paper and plaster paneling, installed in the large salon of the second floor, had hidden the original wooden "*par y nudillo*" structure, with knot-work ornaments, of the roof. The house was in an acceptable state of conservation when work began to turn it into a residential building with eleven "suite"-type rooms. The recovery of the original spatiality of the salon was one of the first jobs of intervention undertaken in the house. The dining room, which opens onto the patio, was placed in the republican wing. The ceiling that had been in the main salon was installed in this space. Two mural paintings, found in the stairway space and the second-storey vestibule, were carefully restored.

The treatment of the main patio, with a linear fountain bordered by palm trees, was inspired by Arab-style patios. The swimming pool was located in the rear garden, which has a lawn and flower beds.

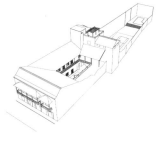 

Aerial view and main façade

Page 104, longitudinal plan
Page 105, longitudinal plan

HOUSE ON CALLE SAN PEDRO MÁRTIR

Cartagena 1994/1995

This is a "low", one-storey house, located in the San Diego district of the walled city. Originally, it only had one front section, which extended to the garden by means of a shed. When the present owners acquired the property it was completely covered by buildings and an attic with a wooden structure had been built above the front.

To remodel the house so that it would serve once more as a home all of the additions were removed and the front section was freed, where a salon which opens onto the patio was placed and a small attic was built. At the rear of the property a new two-storey block was constructed, in which the dining room and main bedroom were located. A small open space at the back allows air to circulate through these spaces. A "Roman" bath was installed on one side of the patio. The water which supplies it gushes forth and flows down the side wall.

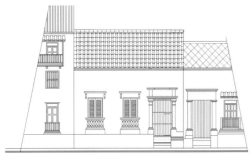

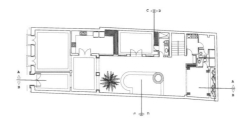

Plans of main façade and ground floor

HOUSE ON CALLE DE LAS DAMAS

Cartagena 1995

This two-storey house must have formerly had a traditional "U"-shaped layout with a side patio. The addition of a fourth section formed the present central patio. With the deterioration of time the rear section was completely lost: only a few vestiges remained. In the front section the original spaces of the entrance hall, stairway and the large second-storey salon with a balcony on the façade had been conserved. The intervention in this body included the restoration of the "*par y nudillo*" structure of the roof, based on the surviving vestiges of tie-beams with knot-work ornaments. The plaster and original colors of the old walls were restored.

To form the central patio the three remaining sections were restored, conserving the surviving remnants. The ground floor was worked so as to allow all of the spaces to open onto the patio. In the rear section an open space was placed at the back and the swimming pool was located within that space. The bedrooms were installed on the second floor of one of the lateral sections and the rear one. A terrace was built over the other lateral section to enlarge the spatiality of the patio. A terrace-watchtower was placed at the top of the third storey of the rear section.

OFFICES OF SEGUROS MAPFRE FIRM, CALLE DE LA INQUISICIÓN

Cartagena 1995

This corner house dates back to the 18th century and was reformed in the 19th and 20th centuries. The republican-style ornamentation of the façade and the interior spaces is a relic of those interventions. Around 1930 the house was the seat of the Masonic Lodge. It has a central patio which is reached by an entrance hall centered on one of the axes. The patio is bordered by the arches of the ground floor. The corridor of the second-storey rests on wooden brackets and columns. On this floor there are arches only in front of the main stairway.

During one of the previous interventions the rear section was raised to four stories; balconies resting on cement brackets, with "little roofs" of the same material, were built; the traditional eave was removed; and an "attic" which partly concealed the ceramic tile roof was installed. Some remnants of the old wooden corner balcony were found.

The intervention, intended to turn the house into offices, conserved elements of the different periods—colonial and republican. Stores were opened on the street side of the ground floor. The offices were placed in three of the sections of the second floor. The large salon which occupies one of the fronts of the house was restored and converted into a conference room and social center. In the rear section, starting on the second floor and finishing in a terrace, there is an apartment for the executives of the company which owns the building. The work restored all of the cement ornamentation of the façades of the house.

HOUSE ON CALLE DE LA INQUISICIÓN

Cartagena 1995/1996

This two-storey house with a mezzanine is located near the Plaza de Bolívar and has a typical "U"-shaped floor plan around a side patio. It was harmed by a previous intervention and was in an advanced state of deterioration. An initial examination led to the discovery of some very important features, for example, the columns at the entrance with stone capitals that have carved flower motifs, unique in the city. These capitals had been covered in cement. Vestiges of the old watchtower were also found. Most of the works of intervention in this house were aimed at restoring the original spaces and features. One of the first jobs to be done was the relocation and reconstruction of the main stairway. The structure of the salon was rebuilt on the basis of the surviving vestiges. The stone capitals were carefully restored. The three surviving water cisterns in the patio were conserved and the watchtower was reconstructed. A terrace was built in the rear wing, which lacked a roof, and the swimming pool was placed on one side of it. The red color applied to the façade of the house was taken from vestiges found in the main patio.

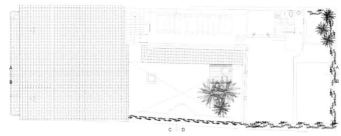

Roof plan

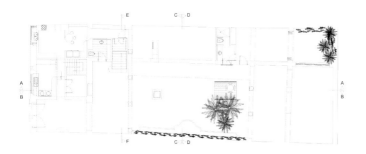

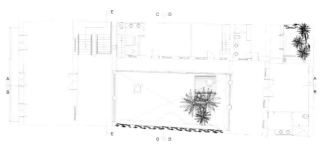

HOUSE OF COUNT OF PESTAGUA
CALLE SANTO DOMINGO

Cartagena 1996/1997

This house, of prime importance, forms part of a group of four houses whose façades are of the same height and have the same kinds of doorways. They probably belonged to the Conde de Pestagua (Count of Pestagua). It occupies a very lengthy property which has a second front on the Plaza de la Artillería, where coaches must have entered the ample garden. The house is built around a long, narrow central patio. The front section has the mezzanine that characterized big merchants' houses and a large salon with a balcony that occupies the whole front of the house. The rear section and one of the lateral ones had three stories from the beginning, a feature found in very few houses in the old part of the city. Among the other special features of the house there is the large stairway and a vaulted water cistern with reliefs in the wall that faces the corridor. Previous interventions had done harm to the original values of the house and they had to be restored.

The house was subdivided into three apartments of generous proportions which share the large salon as a common space. The restoration of the original elements included the recuperation of the mural paintings and the drawings of ships on the walls, common features of the great colonial houses of Cartagena. The large garden was turned into a recreational area, with a swimming pool and a sports ground. The second front of the property was converted into an entranceway and parking space for vehicles.

"EL PORVENIR" BUILDING, CALLE DEL PORVENIR

Cartagena 1996/1997

This apartment building was formerly known as the "Ganem del Porvenir" building. It was built over the remains of an old colonial house, of which the two first-floor patios, surrounded by arcades, had survived. Three additional stories were constructed on top of the arches. They had concrete columns without iron reinforcement bars, mixed slabs supported on concrete beams and wooden floors placed on a thin layer of mortar. The roof was originally of zinc. This project dates back to 1942 and is thought to be by the architect Rafael García Rey, who was responsible for several works in the historic center of Cartagena de Indias.

The intervention concentrated on recovering the residential use of the building, with 19 apartments of different kinds, some single and others duplex. The main façade and the arcades of the interior patio were completely conserved. The main stairway was relocated and a second stairway was built in the second patio. The structure was completely reinforced. The front section was covered with a two-slope ceramic tile roof. In the rear part the zinc roof tiles were replaced by a flat roof that serves as a terrace for the whole group of apartments. To ensure privacy, the apartments which give onto the interior corridors have "*Mudéjar*"-type balcony lattices cast in concrete from old moulds found in the city.

Longitudinal cross section plan
Pages 134 and 135, plans of ground, second, third and fourth floors

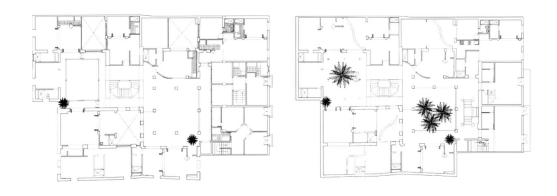

HOUSE ON CALLE DEL CURATO

Cartagena 1996/1997

The only parts of the original house that had been conserved were the front section, with a lateral entrance hall; an ample corridor with arcades in front of the patio; and the salon on the front. An enormous mango tree growing within the property became one of the central elements of the conversion of the house into a residence. The reproduction of the features of the side patio provided the criteria for the development of the whole intervention.

Two bedrooms were placed in the front section with their bathrooms on the two "mezzanines", which are reached by interior stairways. The rest of the house was organized into a two-storey-high section with two arms, which defines the spatiality of the patio. The ground floor of this section serves as the social area. A masonry stairway, built into one of the lateral walls, leads to the second storey, where a metal bridge gives access to the main bedroom. A second metal bridge connects with the terrace-watchtower located above this bedroom. The design of the swimming pool incorporated the mango tree.

The final result of this intervention is a house that is open, informal and adapted to the hot climate.

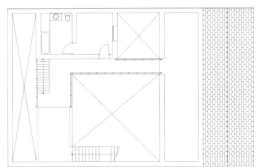

Plan of ground floor

HOUSE ON CALLE DE LA FACTORÍA

Cartagena 1997/1998

The original colonial house only had the front section, which was enlarged in the republican period to acquire an "L"-shaped plan with a side patio. From that period date the doorway and the fluted neo-classical columns that border the patio.

Its conversion into a residence involved the restoration of all of the old elements, both colonial and republican, including the roofs. The rear section of two stories was partly extended to the back of the lot, to house the service areas. A terrace-watchtower with a "Jacuzzi" occupies part of the third floor of this section. The large swimming pool covers a good part of the side patio which was shaped by the reforms.

HOUSE ON CALLE DE LOS ESTRIBOS

Cartagena 1999

Of the original structure of this two-storey house, there had only survived part of the front section, which had been completely transformed and covered by a roof of asbestos-cement tiles. In the rear part of the property the ruins of an old shed were found. The façade had suffered a lot of alteration. Most of the existing walls had to be demolished in order to remodel the house. Of the colonial structure, only the façade and the lateral walls remained. On the ground floor of the front section a new space for the "*zaguán*" (entrance hall) was defined in the place where the original one probably stood. The salon, dining room and kitchen were also placed on that floor. A lateral stairway provides access to a mezzanine that serves as the study. The whole of this space opens, through an arch, onto the main patio, where the swimming pool was placed. An examination of the façade led to the discovery and restoration of the original openings for the windows. A new, three-storey block was built in the rear part to house the bedrooms: it is topped by a terrace. A metal stairway and a bridge connect this block to the main section.

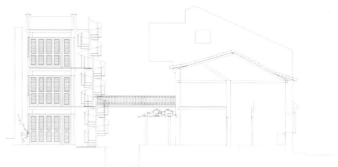

Plan of façade and side cross-section

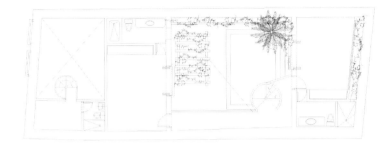

Plan of second floor

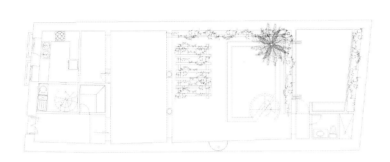

HOUSE ON CALLE DE DON SANCHO

Cartagena 1999/2000

The interior of this two-storey colonial house had been completely demolished. Only the shell of the front section and the lateral walls remained. The original stairway had disappeared. The space of the entrance hall on the ground floor had to be reconstructed and a new stairway designed, which was placed at the point where the property narrows towards the rear.

In this, as in other interventions, the original elements of the front section were restored and the roof was rebuilt. A new three-storey section was built in the back part of the patio: it is crowned by a terrace-watchtower. A garden with a fountain serves as the backdrop to the ground floor of this section. A stream of water falls over the side wall of the patio into a small fountain.

The main bedroom, with its bathroom and dressing room, was installed in the space of the old salon on the second floor. Above this, on the mezzanine, there is a studio.

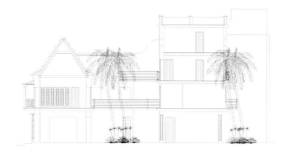

Longitudinal cross-section plan
Page 156, plan of first floor
Page 157, plan of second floor

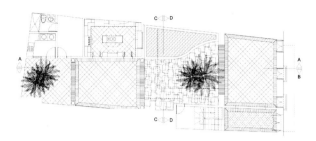

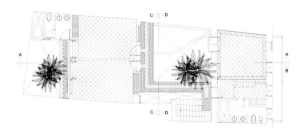

HOUSE ON CALLE DEL COLEGIO

Cartagena 2000

A basic structure made up of two sections in the form of an "L" and a side patio had survived in this two-storey colonial house. The house was transformed into a factory around 1935 and a rear section of four stories was constructed, which closed in the patio: one unusual feature was a freight elevator in the center of the space. At the rear of the property part of the old garden had been conserved. The house had been abandoned for several years, which led to a severe deterioration of the colonial structure.

The main problem faced in the intervention of this house was to ensure that its conversion into a small condominium would make the three resulting homes as independent as possible. The restored colonial structure became a separate home, with a swimming pool on the terrace formed by the roof of the lateral section. The two remaining residences were built on the four floors of the republican building. One of them occupies the whole of the ground floor, which conserves its original 5 meters height and has a swimming pool in the garden. The other, which is reached by a metal stairway located in the main patio, occupies the two floors above it and has a terrace with a swimming pool on the fourth floor.

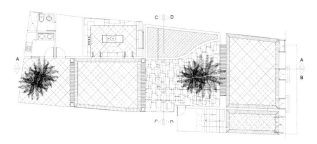

Floor plan of mezzanine

158

CASA LIÉVANO

Bogotá 1979

This house stands in the historic center of Bogotá, a block from the *Plaza de Bolívar*. Its basic structure dates back to the colonial period and it was completely remodeled in the "republican" style in the 19th century. The latter intervention was responsible for the enclosed balconies on the façade and the wood and plaster ornamentation of the interior. This is one of the few examples of a house with a double central patio. A third patio, built in the space of the old garden, is a recent addition.

An entrance hall in the middle of the ground floor leads to the vestibule, which opens onto the main patio, joined to the second patio by a narrow corridor. The main rooms are placed on the second floor, along the facade. The dining room is in the center, between the two patios. The main features of the very simple façade are the enclosed side balconies and the central balconies of the second floor.

The restoration of the house concentrated on removing unsuitable additions and freeing the interior spaces for use as the offices of the Arts Section of the Colombian Institute of Culture. One of the most interesting aspects of the intervention was the research undertaken to determine the colors of the interior and exterior. On the basis of this study the façade was given a color of red and different tones of green, which provoked a controversy because it contradicted a norm, adopted in several cities in the 1950s, that required the use of white for historic houses.

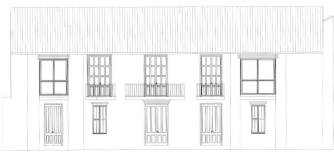

Plan of main façade

MONTES HACIENDA HOUSE – NARIÑO MUSEUM

Bogotá 1997

The Montes hacienda house was the place where Antonio Nariño, one of the leaders of the Colombian independence movement, was imprisoned by the Spanish authorities between the beginning of August, 1803 and June, 1804. The original building of the hacienda had a central patio bordered by corridors, with another two patios, one that served as the entrance and another that was probably used as a garden.

The original kitchen of the hacienda faced the latter patio. The central one is surrounded by glass windows of republican origin. The hacienda has earth and adobe walls.

The intervention aimed at converting the hacienda house into a place that would be suitable for educational and cultural activities. The old parts were completely restored so that their spaces may serve for new uses. The old garden became a site for open-air events and the old kitchen was incorporated into the cafeteria. Earth tones were used on the façade and in the interior spaces.

Plan of main façade

166

HOTEL DE LA ÓPERA

Bogotá 1999

Two houses, constructed in different epochs, were joined to form this 30-room hotel next to the Teatro Colón, the oldest and most distinguished opera house in the city of Bogotá. The outstanding one is a corner house built in the 18th century with earth and adobe walls, arranged around a central patio bordered by three-centered arches resting on square columns on the ground floor and segmented arches resting on round columns on the second.

In the 19th century the main stairway was changed and ornamentation of diverse kinds was added. The second is a republican house of the beginning of the 20th century, which has a side patio and a watchtower above the façade.

As well as integrating the two buildings, the main objective of the intervention was to recover some of the original values and to employ a single architectural language, in this case that of the republican style. In the colonial house the structures of earth and adobe were strengthened and the old structure of the roof was reinforced, without changing its components. The original stone floor of the main patio was recovered. The republican staircase was removed and a new one and an elevator were placed in a central point. The main dining room and the bar were placed on the highest floor of the republican house and in the watchtower: they are supplied from the kitchen by a service lift. The two patios were covered with glass canopies that are in harmony with the character of each house.

In order to fulfill its present use, the bedrooms of the hotel were placed around the patios, in accordance with the traditional plan. The space of the colonial entrance hall was conserved and incorporated into one of the first-floor guest bedrooms. The space used as the dining room on the second floor of the colonial house was converted into the main salon and conserved the large fireplace, the wooden moldings of the walls and the coffered ceiling. The chapel was conserved in its original form.

Cross-section plan

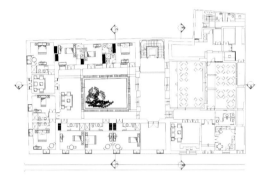

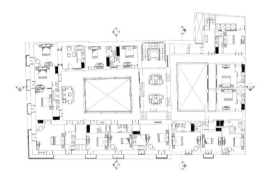

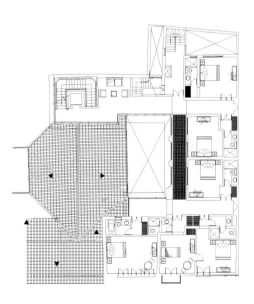

CASA MORALES AND
CASA DEL MARQUÉS DE PORTAGO

Panama City 1996/1997

This four-storey corner house is located in the historic center of Panama City and has a concrete structure resting on the walls of an 18th century colonial house. One special feature are the projecting balconies on the second and third floors. The fourth floor only consisted of a roof, meant to protect the building from the hot sun.

The intervention in the building resulted in four apartments of a generous size, served by a centrally-located stairway and elevator. A bar was placed on the corner of the ground floor. The original elements of the façade were duly restored.

This building with a concrete structure was built on top of the ground floor of an old colonial house, of which there only remained the shell formed by the stone façade, with the window openings and balconies of the different floors, the side walls, the rear wall and, at the back of the property, at the side of a patio, a small watchtower which rises three stories above the level of the roof. In the remodeling into apartments all of these elements were conserved.

A central stairwell with a stairway and elevator serves the three apartments on the first two floors. On the third floor there is a duplex apartment which has a fourth-floor terrace, with an entrance to the watchtower. In the restoration of the façade an emphasis was given to the original stone elements.

LAS BÓVEDAS RESTAURANT

Panama City 1998

Las Bóvedas ("The Vaults") is an 18th century military construction that formed part of the main colonial fortress of Panama City. It is made up of six vaulted rectangular spaces that are joined by a horseshoe-shaped platform that ends in a ramp, forming a medium-sized plaza which connects, in turn, with a park. The building was reformed several years ago and some spaces had been converted into a restaurant, a use which was conserved in the new intervention.

The restaurant occupies four of the six surviving vaults. The restoration work undertook, in the first place, to eliminate the wooden floors that had been built in the past. In the new plan the entrance and the kitchen were placed in the second vault. On one of its sides are the restaurant and the bar, which are connected with the kitchen through the service areas. The storerooms and toilets lie on the other side of the entrance.

The brick vaults were completely restored, along with the ocher–colored plastering of the walls.

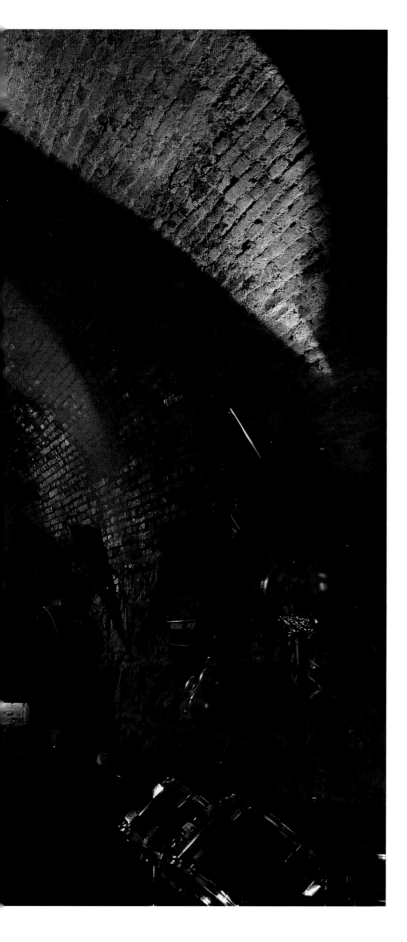

HOTEL COLOMBIA

Panama City 1998

This hotel was constructed on a corner in the historic center of Panama City, in front of the Parque de Bolívar. This property previously held a number of houses that had been turned into a hotel which lodged Colombians who visited the city to undergo treatments by U.S. doctors. Around 1937 the owners of the hotel commissioned a Panamanian architect to construct a new building for the hotel on the same site.

The result was a four-storey building with a terrace whose symmetrical façade displays an eclectic mixture of neo-colonial and Moorish elements. A projecting balcony running along the second floor is covered by a small roof. The fourth floor projects from the plane of the façade and rests on concrete brackets. Two small towers crown this arrangement. On the terrace a series of free columns were found, which may have been meant for a future enlargement.

The building had been empty for a number of years before it was acquired for conversion into 16 new apartments. On the ground floor the store that served as the hotel´s restaurant survived and it serves the same function today. A central stairwell formed by the stairway and elevator separates it from the garages. The restaurant´s kitchen, storerooms and the communal laundry room of the residences were placed at the rear.

The floor plan conserved the lay-out of the corridors of the old hotel, which serve the five apartments on the second and third floors. Three larger apartments, one a duplex, were installed on the fourth floor. The terrace was used as a communal area, and a small swimming pool was placed there. The free columns were restored and are used as supports for flower beds.

NEW WORK

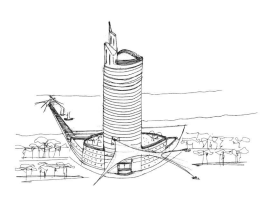

TWO-FAMILY BUILDING, CEDRITOS NEIGHBORHOOD

Bogotá 1974

Twin residences were laid out on a big lot in the north of Bogotá. Each one is developed around a patio which separates the garages and stairways from the service rooms. An area of circulation branches off from the central entrance and runs around the whole of the ground floor, ending in the dining room. The living room, located in the center of the house, a few steps below the circulation area, opens onto both the garden and the patio.

On the second floor the stairway ends in a corridor that serves as a bridge between the two-storey-high space of the living room and the patio. The main bedroom, placed along the façade, can completely open onto the space of the living room, whose canoe-shaped roof has a skylight. The other bedrooms, with their respective bathrooms, occupy the rest of this floor.

A transparent roof, resting on wooden beams, was used in the garages. In the exterior the differentiation of the volumes was highlighted in order to emphasize their orthogonal character.

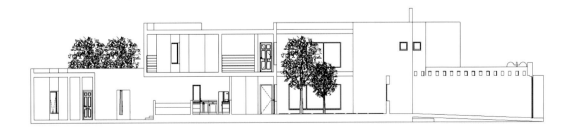

Cross-section plan

HOUSE IN GUAYMARAL

Bogotá 1983

This house was built on a rural property near the Guaymaral airport, north of the city of Bogotá. The arrangement of its floor plan is relatively simple: a lateral entranceway opens onto the vestibule-dining room. On the left side are found the study and salon, separated by a single-flight stairway. The kitchen and laundry patio are on the right side. On the second floor the stairway ends in a bridge which provides access to the main bedroom.

The complex spatial arrangement of the house is based on the intersection of two volumes – a rectangular one in brick and an another "L"-shaped one – with a diagonal wooden structure from which a rhomboidal section projects. On the entranceway side the façade is worked entirely in wood. On the opposite façade brick is inserted within the wooden rhomboids of the structure. Part of the inclined planes that are created by this volume serve as a glass roof in the vestibule and salon. The roof of the upper part is made of a black asbestos-cement "shingle".

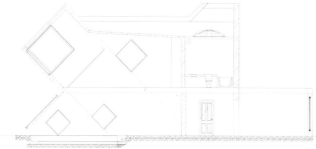

Cross-section plan

188

SANTA ROSA PLAZA BUILDING

Bogotá 1986

This five-storey-high building contains 32 apartments and occupies the longer side of an ample "L"-shaped property situated in the "Country Club" district of Bogotá. To conserve the trees on the site all sides of the building were set back from the borders of the property. In the remaining area a semi-basement with a squash court was built, whose volume rises a little above street level. The car park is in the basement. Its 4 meters height allows for storage rooms above the cars and also for the hanging concrete flower beds of the patios.

The building has a symmetrical floor plan and is arranged around two open interior patios. A central stairwell and two lateral ones provide access to all of the apartments. A pergola that crosses the patios joins the stairwells on the ground floor. The four corner apartments are alike.

They have an octagonal entrance vestibule with a diagonal approach, which connects with the dining room, living room and study. The service area is placed alongside the dining room, on the longitudinal axis of the building. A corridor provides access to the vestibule of the bedrooms, which is also octagonal. The central apartments have a different lay-out. The apartments on the upper storey have vaulted concrete roofs.

In the exterior treatment use was made of closed surfaces of brick and exposed concrete, with balconies that have metal railings.

Overall floor plan

BUILDING-RESTORATION WORKSHOP

Bogotá 1993

On this property, which faces a pedestrian walkway, there existed a modern-looking house, with a structure of brick buttresses, mud-and-straw walls and a roof of asphalt canvas resting on wooden pillars. The initial idea of the project was to remodel this house but the focus was changed when it became evident that the structure was too precarious. It was thus decided to build a small, four-storey building intended to house a residence and a workshop for the restoration of paintings.

Two stores were placed on the ground floor, along with the entrance to the upper floors. Part of the workshop was placed on the second floor, which also holds the private stairway to the residence. The third floor is shared by the workshop and part of the home (dining room, kitchen and patio). A spiral staircase leads to the fourth floor, where the living room, main bedroom and a broad terrace that occupies part of the façade are found.

The wall of the façade was worked in adobe made in the surroundings of Bogotá, with intercalated courses of *"racilla"* brick, and was crowned by brick cornices. The spaces of the uppermost floor are covered by concrete vaults that were originally covered with yellow ceramic tiles. The interior of the vaults were painted in bright colors and their edges have moldings that conceal the lighting system. In general, very simple and economical finishes were applied: floors in ceramic tiles and smoothed cement, skirtboard in cement and forged iron for grilles and railings.

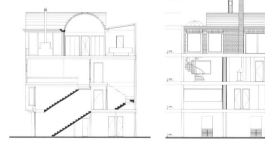

Cross sections of sides and main façade of building
page 200, plans of ground,
second, third and fourth floors

COUNTRY HOUSE IN EL ROSAL

El Rosal, Cundinamarca 1996

A diagonally-placed door provides access to a vestibule-corridor which separates the two sections of the house. In one of them is found the ample living-dining room, kitchen and main bedroom. In the other are the remaining bedrooms, with their respective bathrooms. A stairway leads to the study, which opens onto the living room.

The house, built with brick walls, has a large roof of ceramic tiles which rests on a thin layer of concrete supported by a structure of wooden logs. The geo-textile material used to uphold the concrete was exposed to view in the interior and gives a special texture to the ceiling of the house. The interior and exterior walls were painted in ocher and earth tones.

VILLA FÁTIMA RESIDENTIAL COMPLEX

Envigado, Antioquia 1986

This is the main house of a complex of nine houses designed for the members of a large family. Care was taken with the landscaping and environmental aspects of the ample terrain, a sloping one that has two gullies full of vegetation. There are, in all, four different types of houses, which follow the same basic criteria and were built with the same materials: load bearing structures in concrete, exterior walls in an adobe of special dimensions with intermediate brick strips, brick cornices and roofs of enameled blue ceramic tiles.

The adobe blocks and roof tiles were fabricated on the site.

This house is built around an octagonal vestibule that leads to the different functional areas. Facing the entrance is the main salon, which is completely open to the vista of the distant landscape. The dining room and the services zones are located on the left side. To the right of the salon is the library. An area of circulation branches off from the vestibule and leads to a second vestibule, which is meant for the bedrooms. On both ends of the house there are semi-basements. The garages are found in one of them and the swimming pool, with its complementary services, in the other.

The roofs of the main spaces show diverse treatments. The salon has a four-slope roof which rests on a traditional wooden "*par y nudillo*" structure. The dining room and library have canoe-shaped concrete ceilings and the vestibules are crowned by cupolas. This allows for a succession of interior spaces of different shapes and heights, inspired by the character of Islamic architecture.

Plan of ground floor

HOUSE IN SANTA CLARA

Panama City 1986

This vacation home stands on a large property near
the sea, in the Santa Clara urban development in
Panama City. The center of the design is a spacious
area that serves as an informal living room, open on
both sides to receive the sea breezes. A corridor,
covered by small concrete vaults, borders two sides
of this space, one of which leads to the bedrooms.
On one side of the entrance there is a long strip
where the garages, kitchen and a formal salon-dining
room are located. A stairway leads to the second
floor of this strip, where the main bedroom with its
complementary areas is found.

The two-slope roofs, in ceramic tiles, of the salon and
the bedroom have a moderate inclination. The
volume of the main bedroom stands out by virtue of
its greater height and horizontal shape.

WORK IN PROGRESS

HOUSE ON CALLE DE LAS DAMAS

Cartagena 2003

Of the original one-storey house there survived the front section, with the elements characteristic of its typology: a lateral entrance hall, a corridor with a central column facing the patio and a salon with part of the simple "*par y nudillo*" roof structure, which lacks, however, the conventional canoe-shaped cross section. The property occupied by the house had been subdivided and a two-storey building, connected to the neighboring house, was built. This part was acquired once more and the property was restored to its original size. Two surviving features of the original building were conserved: a palm tree and the old water cistern.

The front section, whose structure was rebuilt on the basis of the surviving remnants, was converted into the living room of the new residence. The dining room and kitchen were placed on the ground floor of the two-storey lateral section. The patio was converted into a large swimming pool which runs beyond the old boundary wall of the garden and is partly covered by a fairly transparent wooden "deck" which ends in a "Jacuzzi" at the back of the property. A "wall of water" interacts with the swimming pool. A stairway built into the lateral wall of the patio leads to the main bedroom by means of a bridge which bends to reach a terrace located above the corridor of the front section.

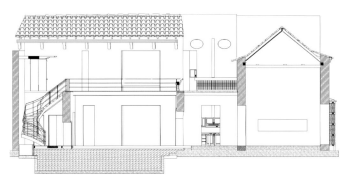

Cross-section plan

218

HOUSE IN PUNTA PACÍFICO

Panama City 2003

The main space which defines the interior and exterior ordering of this house is a very large atrium, with a pool of water in the center and two rows of palms on the sides, covered by a brick vault whose center rises to a height of nine meters. The entrance door is located on one side, and protected by a wooden pergola upheld by cables. On the opposite side is the big salon. Two vaulted volumes stand out on the right side. One of them is the main stairway and the other is a den (or informal living room), next to the main salon.

On the opposite side there is a rectangular volume with a two-slope roof, separated from the former by a corridor. The dining room and services area lie on the ground floor and the bedrooms on the second, which are connected to the stairway by means of a bridge that crosses the central atrium. The exteriors of the house are treated with exposed brick.

PUNTA PACÍFICO BUILDING

Punta Pacífico, Panama 2003

This apartment building is thirty stories high. The car parks occupy the first four floors. The entrance vestibule is on the ground floor, with panoramic elevators and the main stairway. Each floor has two large apartments on either side of a great central void crossed by the bridges which lead to the stairways and the elevators. Each apartment has an ample balcony that completely spans one of the façades.

On each balcony there is a swimming pool that projects from the façade. The arrangement of these swimming pools follows an alternating pattern, which is repeated on every other floor.

The concrete structure of this building is exposed on all sides and in the interior voids. The alternating volumes of the swimming pools stand out from it.

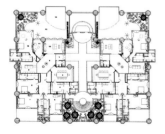

Overall floor plan
Plans, next page:
Floor plans of ground floor, car park
and alternating floors of apartments

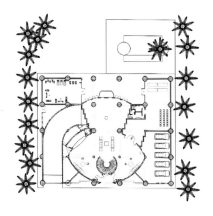

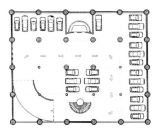

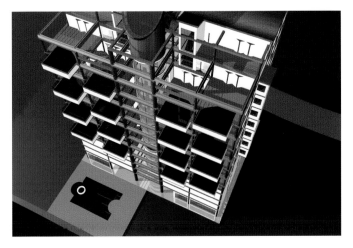

HOUSE ON EAST COAST

Costa del Este, Panama 2003

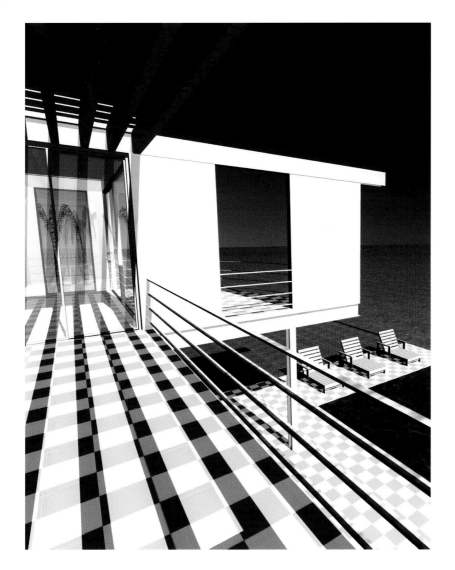

This house is arranged around an ample two-storey-high central space, which is treated as a pool of water. In the front of the house are the entrance, the garages, the guest bedroom and the main stairway. On one side of the central space there is a palm garden and on the opposite one, the kitchen and the services area. The salon, dining room and informal living room are placed on the side opposite to the entrance and are reached by means of a zigzagging wooden bridge that crosses the pool of water.

The area of circulation of the second floor, where the bedrooms and study are located, is achieved through another wooden bridge which does not interrupt the spatial continuity of the main areas of the house. Two terraces with a steel deck face the bedroom area and the studio. The swimming room is at the edge of the property, facing the sea.

The metallic structure of the house, painted white, serves as a frame for the smooth brick surfaces of the same color. The central space has a slightly vaulted roof, which is separated from the flat roofs of the sides.

Plan of ground floor

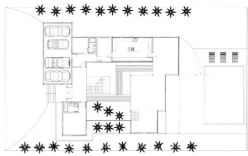

CHRONOLOGY

ÁLVARO BARRERA-HERRERA

STUDIES

1972   Universidad de América. Bogotá, Colombia.

SPECIALIST STUDIES

1974-1975 Spanish Institute of Tourism. Planning of
         Tourist Sites, Madrid, Spain.

1973-1975 Institute of Hispanic Culture.
         Restoration of monuments, Madrid, Spain.

1976   Pontificia Universidad Javeriana.
        Restoration of architectural monuments.
        Bogotá, Colombia.

1981   School of Conservation, Restoration and
        Museum Work. Restoration of
        monuments. Bogotá, Colombia.

SPECIALIST COURSES

1971   Universidad de América and the NASA.
        Design of habitat in space modules.
        Bogotá, Colombia.

1971   National Apprenticeship Service (SENA).
        Construction and direction of works.
        Bogotá, Colombia.

1976   National Tourism Corporation. Seminar on
        Tourism and Development. Bogotá,
        Colombia.

1976   Pontificia Universidad Javeriana.
        Management of works. Bogotá, Colombia.

1975   Institute of Hispanic Culture. Ministry of
        Information and Tourism. 12th Course on
        tourism for Latin American graduate
        professionals and technicians. Madrid, Spain.

1976   Higher School of Public Administration
        (ESAP). Evaluation of projects, Bogotá,
        Colombia.

PARTICIPATION IN PROFESSIONAL EVENTS

1978   Inter-American Seminar on Inventory of
        Historic Buildings, Lima, Peru

1979   7th Colombian Biennial of Architecture.

1979   Congress on Restoration, Mexico.

1981   8th Colombian Biennial of Architecture,
        Fourth prize (modular house).

1979   Biennial of Quito. House in Bogotá.

1979   Annual meeting of the Institute of
        Conservation and Restoration of Rome.
        Colombian representative.

1980   Meeting of Andrés Bello Agreement.
        Representative of Colombian government.
        Santiago, Chile.

1980   Meeting of experts in museum work.
        Colombian delegate. Lima, Peru.

1981   Congress of planners, guest speaker,
        Mexico City, Mexico.

1981   Representative of Colombian government
        at the signing of the Hispano-Colombian
        Cultural Agreement, Madrid, Spain.

CONSULTANT WORK

1980   Consultant for the restoration of the
        historic center of the city of Potosí, Bolivia,
        on behalf of the Unesco.

TEACHING EXPERIENCE

1976   Universidad Piloto de Colombia. Advisor
        on workshop on tourism. Third semester.

1976   Universidad de América. Theses advisor.

1976 and 1978 Universidad Católica de Colombia.
        Workshop Professor, 6th and 9th semesters.

1976   Universidad Externado de Colombia. Director of theses (tourism planning).

1976   Universidad Nacional, Advisor, 10th semester.

1977-1978 Universidad Externado de Colombia. Director of research. Professor of hotel planning.

1976 - 1977 Universidad la Gran Colombia. Workshop 7 and 8.

1972   Workshop on tourism in the hotel sector. Cúcuta, Colombia.

PUBLICATIONS

1974   *Escala* (magazine), "*Cabañas turísticas*" (Tourist cabañas).

1977   Book published by the Committee for the Restoration of Honda, Colombia. *Estudio sobre el casco antiguo de la ciudad de Honda* (Study of the historic center of the city of Honda).

1976/1982 *Anuario de Arquitectura en Colombia.* (Yearbook of Colombian Architecture). Projects published in the following volumes: No. 5, 1976; No. 7, 1978; No. 9, 1980; No. 10, 1981; No. 11, 1982.

1981   *Revista del Centro de Estudios de la Arquitectura A.R.S.* ("A.R.S." - Magazine of the Center of Studies of Architecture). Santiago, Chile.

1982   *Revista Proa* (magazine), No. 306. Bogotá, Colombia.

1982   Publication, conference and talks. Congress of Architects. "*Recuperación del hábitat*" (Recuperation of habitat). Manizales, Colombia.

1985   *Historia de la Arquitectura en Colombia* (History of Architecture in Colombia). Works included: *Convento de San Agustín, Tunja.* (Monastery of San Agustín, Tunja). *Reintegración arquitectónica.* (Architectural reintegration). "*Casa modular", arquitectura moderna.* ("Modular house", modern architecture). Published by: Colombian Ministry of Foreign Relations, Universidad de los Andes.

1986   *Revista Proa*, No. 305. Bogotá.

1986   *Escala*, No. 130. Bogotá.

1986   *Escala,* No. 131. Bogotá.

PROFESSIONAL AFFILIATIONS

1972   Partner of the Rojas, Barrera, González firm.

1972   Partner of the Proarco Ltda. firm.

PROFESSIONAL POSTS

1972   Architect of the Projects Division. Colombian National Tourism Corporation.

1972-1973 Director of works, tourist circuit of Boyacá, Colombia (Leave for studies abroad). National Tourism Corporation.

1973   Director of Supervision Division. National Tourism Corporation.

1975 y 1977 Director of Projects Division. National Tourism Corporation.

1975   Assistant director of operations (temporary). National Tourism Corporation.

1975   Member of the Council on National Monuments, representing the National Tourism Corporation.

1976/1981 Director of Cultural Heritage section and Assistant Director of the Colombian Institute of Culture (Colcultura) in the field of heritage.

1978   CEO of the Inecol Ltda. firm (Industrias Cerámicas de Colombia).

1978-1982 Director of Works. Foundation for the Conservation and Restoration of the Colombian Cultural Heritage.

Firm of Álvaro Barrera arquitectos asociados, in partnership with the architect Gloria Patricia Martínez.

Office of projects and researches for the restoration of historic centers. Director and proprietor, 1982 to present.

Firm of Barrera y Barrera arquitectos consultores-restauradores, Panama, to present..

SELECTED PROJECTS

Cloister and church of San Agustín
Location: Tunja, Colombia
Work realized: design and direction
of work
Date: 1978/1984

House on Calle de Don Sancho
Location: Cartagena, Colombia
Work realized: design, building and
adaptation to apartments
Date: 1982

Casa de los Barcos
Location: Cartagena, Colombia
Work realized: design, restoration
and adaptation, in partnership with
the architect Gloria Patricia Martínez
Date: 1984

Casa Gastelbondo
Location: Cartagena, Colombia
Work realized: design, restoration
and adaptation, in partnership with
the architect Gloria Patricia Martínez
Date: 1986

Corner house Calle de la Mantilla
and Calle del Curato
Location: Cartagena, Colombia
Work realized: design, restoration
and adaptation, in partnership with
the architect Gloria Patricia Martínez
Date: 1988

House on Calle de la Estrella
Location: Cartagena, Colombia
Work realized: design and
restoration, in partnership with the
architect Gloria Patricia Martínez
Date: 1989/1990

House on Calle Tumbamuertos
Location: Cartagena, Colombia
Work realized: restoration, in
partnership with the architect Gloria
Patricia Martínez
Date: 1991

House on Calle Tumbamuertos
Location: Cartagena, Colombia
Work realized: design and
restoration, in partnership with the
architect Gloria Patricia Martínez
Date: 1992

House on Calle del Curato
Location: Cartagena, Colombia
Work realized: design and
restoration, in partnership with the
architect Gloria Patricia Martínez
Date: 1992

House on Calle de la Mantilla
Location: Cartagena, Colombia
Work realized: design and
restoration, in partnership with the
architect Gloria Patricia Martínez
Date: 1992/1993

House on Calle de Santo Domingo
Location: Cartagena, Colombia
Work realized: design and restoration
of colonial house
Date: 1992/1993

Corner house on Calle de Mantilla
Location: Cartagena, Colombia
Work realized: design and
restoration, in partnership with the
architect Gloria Patricia Martínez
Date: 1993/1994

Hotel Santa Teresa de Jesís
Location: Cartagena, Colombia
Work realized: design, restoration
and construction
Date: 1995/1997

House on Calle de Santo Domingo
Location: Cartagena, Colombia
Work realized: design and
restoration of colonial house
Date: 1994/1995

House on Calle San Pedro Mártir
Location: Cartagena, Colombia
Work realized: design and
restoration, in partnership with the
architect Gloria Patricia Martínez
Date: 1994/1995

House on Calle de las Damas
Location: Cartagena, Colombia
Work realized: design and
restoration, in partnership with the
architect Gloria Patricia Martínez
Date: 1995

House for the "Seguros Mapfre" firm
Location: Cartagena, Colombia
Work realized: design and
restoration
Date: 1995

House on Calle de la Inquisición
Location: Cartagena, Colombia
Work realized: design and
restoration, in partnership with the
architect Gloria Patricia Martínez
Date: 1995/1996

Conde Pestagua House
Location: Cartagena, Colombia
Work realized: design and
restoration, in partnership with the
architect Gloria Patricia Martínez
Date: 1996/1997

"El Porvenir" building
Location: Cartagena, Colombia
Work realized: design and
restoration
Date: 1996/1997

House on Calle del Curato
Location: Cartagena, Colombia
Work realized: design and
restoration, in partnership with the
architect Gloria Patricia Martínez
Date: 1996/1997

House on Calle de la Factoría
Location: Cartagena, Colombia
Work realized: design and
restoration, in partnership with the
architect Gloria Patricia Martínez
Date: 1994/1996

House on Calle de los Estribos
Location: Cartagena, Colombia
Work realized: design and
restoration, in partnership with the
architect Gloria Patricia Martínez
Date: 1997/1998

House on Calle de Don Sancho
Location: Cartagena, Colombia
Work realized: design and
restoration, in partnership with the
architect Gloria Patricia Martínez
Date: 1999/2000

House on Calle del Colegio
Location: Cartagena, Colombia
Work realized: design and
construction
Date: 1999/2000

Casa Liévano
Location: Bogotá, Colombia
Work realized: design and
construction
Date: 1979

Montes Hacienda house – Nariño
Museum
Location: Bogotá, Colombia
Work realized: design and
restoration
Date: 1997

Hotel de la Ópera
Location: La Candelaria district,
Bogotá, Colombia
Work realized: design and
construction
Date: 1999

Casa Morales
Location: Panama City, Panama
Work realized: design, construction
and restoration
Date: 1996

Casa Marqués de Portago
Location: Panama City, Panama
Work realized: design, construction
and restoration
Date: 1997

"Las Bóvedas" restaurant
Location: Panama City, Panama
Work realized: design and
restoration
Date: 1998

Hotel Colombia
Location: Panama City, Panama
Work realized: design, construction
and restoration, Restauro S.A. firm
Date: 1997/1999

Bifamiliar barrio Cedritos (Two-family
development, Cedritos district)
Location: Bogotá, Colombia
Work realized: design and construction
Date: 1976

House in Guaymaral
Location: Guaymaral, Colombia
Work realized: design and
construction
Date: 1983

Santa Rosa Plaza building
Location: Bogotá, Colombia
Work realized: design and
construction
Date: 1991/1992

Building-Restoration Workshop
Location: Bogotá, Colombia
Work realized: design and
construction
Date: 1993

El Rosal country house
Location: El Rosal, Colombia
Work realized: design and
construction
Date: 1996

Villa Fátima family complex
Location: Envigado, Colombia
Work realized: design and
architectural direction of six homes
Date: 1994/1995

House in Santa Clara
Location: Santa Clara, Panama
Work realized: design and
architectural direction
Date: 1991/1992

Building on Calle 86
Location: Bogotá, Colombia
Work realized: design
Date: 1987

Building on Calle 94
Location: Bogotá, Colombia
Work realized: design
Date: 1987

Rancho Alegre rural complex
Location: Sopó, Colombia
Work realized: design
Date: 1987

Cañaveralejo building
Location: Bogotá, Colombia
Work realized: design
Date: 1987

Costa Bella housing development
Location: Bogotá, Colombia
Work realized: design
Date: 1987

Andalucía country house
Location: Subachoque, Colombia
Work realized: design and construction
Date: 1991

Edificio 82
Location: Bogotá, Colombia
Work realized: design and construction
Date: 1994/1994

Hacienda Tasue
Location: Subachoque, Colombia
Work realized: design and construction
Date: 1996/1997

Hotel Timanco
Location: Pitalito, Colombia
Work realized: supervision
Date: 1974

Parador de Bordones tourist lodge
Location: Salto de Bordones, Colombia
Work realized: direction and construction
Date: 1973

Hotel Yalconia
Location. San Agustín, Colombia
Work realized: direction of project
Date: 1973

Hotel Guimaura
Location: Riohacha, Colombia
Work realized: direction of work and project of
enlargement
Date: 1973

Tourist lodge, Desierto de La Candelaria
Location: Desierto de la Candelaria, Colombia
Work realized: design
Date: 1973

Hostelry El Bosque
Location: Cúcuta, Colombia
Work realized: enlargement and re-adaptation
Date: 1973

San Andrés Tourist Center
Location: Bahía Sardinas, Island of San Andrés,
Colombia
Work realized: design
Date: 1973

Tourist and information center
Location: Cartagena, Colombia
Work realized: design
Date: 1973

San Ignacio restaurant
Location: Tunja, Colombia
Work realized: restoration and adaptation
Date: 1974

Quinta de San Pedro Alejandrino (country estate
where Bolívar passed his final days)
Location: Santa Marta, Colombia
Work realized: control, supervision and restoration
Date: 1974

Hotel Santa Clara
Location: Cartagena, Colombia
Work realized: initial design, in association with the
architect Carlos Campuzano and Roberto de la Vega
Date: 1974

Hotel Estación
Location: Buenaventura, Colombia
Work realized: design
Date: 1974

Hotel in Tumaco
Location: Tumaco, Colombia
Work realized: consultancy, design and direction
Date: 1974

Cartagena International Marina
Location: Cartagena, Colombia
Work realized: design
Date: 1976

San Andrés Marina
Location: San Andrés Island, Colombia
Work realized: consultancy, design and direction

Elías Muvdi Park
Location: Barranquilla, Colombia
Work realized: direction and design
Date: 1976

Hotel Charlotte
Location: Cartagena, Colombia
Work realized: design and construction
Date: 2000

STUDIES AND INVESTIGATIONS

Study of lodges and lookout points in areas of tourist
development
Date: 1973

Study of types of tourist cabañas and their
optimization
Date: 1973

Analysis of zones for camping
Date: 1973

COMPETITIONS

Gilberto Alzate Avendaño Theater
Location: Bogotá, Colombia
Work realized: design, adaptation of theater house
and planning of block of buildings
Prize awarded: second prize
Date. 1986

1st Triennial of Caribbean Architecture
Date: 2002

Hotel de La Ópera
Location: Bogotá, Colombia
Work realized: design, construction, restoration and
adaptation
Project awarded first prize
Date: 2002